A COMPREHENSIVE GUIDE TO STARTING YOUR OWN ONLINE STORE

A COMPREHENSIVE GUIDE TO STARTING YOUR OWN ONLINE STORE

RWG PUBLISHING

RWG Publishing

CONTENTS

1	Introduction to E-Commerce	1
2	Market Research and Niche Selection	5
3	Creating a Business Plan	8
4	Choosing the Right E-Commerce Platform	10
5	Setting Up Your Online Store	13
6	Product Sourcing and Inventory Management	16
7	Payment Gateways and Security	18
8	Marketing and Customer Acquisition	22
9	Customer Service and Retention	25
10	Analyzing and Optimizing Your Store	28
11	Scaling Your E-Commerce Business	32
12	Legal and Compliance Considerations	35
13	Conclusion and Next Steps	37

Copyright © 2024 by RWG Publishing

All rights reserved. No part of this book may be reproduced in any manner whatsoever without written permission except in the case of brief quotations embodied in critical articles and reviews.

First Printing, 2024

CHAPTER 1

Introduction to E-Commerce

What is e-commerce? E-commerce, also known as electronic commerce, is an online platform that allows businesses and individuals to buy and sell goods and services over the Internet. Using e-commerce, buyers can purchase products that are difficult to find elsewhere. The seller will be able to reap greater profits by selling to customers worldwide online 24/7, rather than in person through a physical storefront that requires them to stay open for trading. E-commerce building blocks are: an online website where products can be showcased and bought electronically, a shopping cart, and an online payment system.

There is no doubt that online shopping has revolutionized the way people buy and sell. Many have entered the online retail market either part-time to supplement their income or as full-time entrepreneurs. If you run a brick-and-mortar store in your community and are looking for additional sales channels to increase your profit margins, e-commerce is the answer.

Definition and Importance of E-Commerce

E-commerce is not a merger relationship between technology and business but, in some aspects, a catalyst for economic growth especially in developing countries. Both private citizens and businesses can benefit in a variety of ways, such as gaining access to new markets, improving productivity, developing new production methods, buying or selling products and services through the internet, and receiving services from government. E-commerce is good for businesses and consumers because digital communications now enable buyers and sellers to interact. It is good for customers because it provides them with more information on which to base their purchase decisions, helps them find the products most suitable for their needs, and reduce their purchasing costs. These activities help in realizing some of the significant values associated with B2B and B2C in creating an e-commerce model.

The term 'e-commerce' or 'electronic commerce' has been defined as any form of business transaction in which the parties interact electronically rather than by physical exchanges or direct physical contact. E-commerce involves information and communications technology such as mobile commerce, electronic funds transfer, supply chain management, internet marketing, online transaction processing, electronic data interchange (EDI), inventory management systems, and automated data collection systems. In e-commerce, the roots can be traced back to 1960 when businesses started using electronic data interchange (EDI) to transfer commercial documents electronically. E-commerce later developed to include all the activities related to ordering, selling, and marketing, using digital communication methods.

Trends and Statistics in the E-Commerce Industry

The population of internet users is rapidly increasing and expected to reach 40 million by 2003 according to Gartner Group.

And those online users are spending over 11 hours per week according to a survey by The Dieringer Research Group. Online shopping is all about services and convenience. Shoppers make purchases via the web to save time, eliminate waiting in line, and find unique merchandise often at a better price. A recent study shows consumers shop online for a variety of reasons, stating, "59% felt it is fun to shop online, 54% enjoyed the ability to surf for items while they also handled personal business, 47% of consumers liked the variety of products and the ability to compare products easily, 45% commented on the time and cost savings and 47% also recognized the convenience of online shopping." How does e-commerce fit into the most recent trends of our world? Be assured its place is critical due to these statements: major Internet competencies are investing billions, retail chains are creating monopoly moguls, as entrepreneurs and retailers use e-commerce as their incentive to businesses. Competitive pricing and global opportunities through electronic mediums, for all businesses, can no longer be delayed. Each point of sale entry website has the opportunity of becoming a sales giant, all 300 million sites attempting to obtain market share.

The e-commerce industry, as stated earlier, is growing at an incredibly fast rate. E-commerce sales and transaction processing are growing at an average annual rate of 20%. And with the increasing penetration of the internet, usage is growing at an average annual rate of approximately 15% over the next ten years. Today, approximately one third of U.S. households have purchased merchandise online and projections indicate that about 70% of the population will do so within the next decade. According to an e-commerce survey conducted by Forrester, the number of Americans making purchases online was 29 million in 2000 and is forecasted to rise to 62 million or 40% of online consumers by 2010. These online consumers will make seven billion transactions totaling nearly $1 trillion in the U.S. while Forrester's base case forecast and annual growth rate of online shoppers is 8% from 2005-2010.

CHAPTER 2

Market Research and Niche Selection

Now that you have a niche, you need to analyze your competition. You're not going to want to sell any products that will be a huge conflict of interest with you, in terms of battling out for who can sell the cheapest products. Find out if you're going to sell products that are truly unique, or are readily available from hundreds of other merchants.

One of the first things you'll need to decide before starting your store is what niche your store will cover. Ask yourself these questions: What are you passionate about? Are there products that you love and want to sell? What type of market are you considering? Do you have a unique niche that no one else is selling in yet? After you answer these questions, your ideal niche is likely to reveal itself. Also, it's always a good idea to look through keyword tools like Google AdWords to see if people are looking to buy the types of products you want to sell. Another tool to consider is eBay itself. You can find out popular products on eBay and possibly find merchandise at wholesale prices for any products that catch your eye. Whatever niche you decide on, you'll want to be passionate about working in it, or else opening your store might be extremely unfulfilling to you.

Conducting Market Research

How much income do they have? What kind of education level, family structure, and working conditions are common among the regular customers you want to attract? How will you communicate with them? Are they sharing personal information online? Furthermore, you will need to look at shopping behaviors - how do they buy, where do they buy? What are the rivalries and interests of your customers? After doing your market research, you should seek to address all of the questions that are related to your products or services, find proper launching dates, future online store locations, and properly estimate the procurement and promotion costs that will go into setting up your new web store.

Before you embark on any endeavor, it is important to know your goals and the steps needed to achieve them. In terms of starting work on setting up a web store, the first thing you need to determine is your target market. It's a simple matter of being sure of whom it is that you want to sell your products to. This will determine what kind of products you want to offer and will set the roadmap for designing your store. Conducting market research is vital work. Understanding your target market - which can be the general online shopping community or a targeted niche segment - it is important that you understand the basics of the people who will be buying your products.

Identifying a Profitable Niche

When doing niche research, it is a good idea to identify pain points in the community that your store would be serving. If you have knowledge or experience in the community already, then you likely already know the pain points. However, if you don't, you need to figure out what the members of the community feel is missing.

One of the most important parts of starting an online store is identifying a profitable niche that you can operate within. Identifying the proper niche helps guide most other decisions you will make in starting your online store. It is generally a good idea to start with a niche that you have some interest in, as you will be spending at least some time with it for the foreseeable future. Once you find a niche that you have some interest in, it is time to apply critical thinking to figure out if it is a viable niche. Remember, you can still own well-defined niches in saturated marketplaces. One of my favorite examples of this is ThinkGeek. They sell only nerdy computer-related gear but they have done very well for themselves because the demand is there.

CHAPTER 3

Creating a Business Plan

E-commerce entities are also going to need to focus on customer service. Because of fierce competition and the online comparison process, it is especially critical to understand how to resonate with and service the customer. Providing personalized experiences, leveraging technology to streamline processes, and communicating with customers across a variety of digital channels should be part of a customer service plan. Technology leveraged to draw and keep customers is not something that is just a benefit for the customer experience. It is a valuable resource for a business as well. By collecting and analyzing data, many business decisions become quite clear, and e-commerce businesses have a wealth of data at their fingertips. They should constantly focus on understanding the users by increasingly studying their online behavior, and respond to their preferences and expectations.

Explain how your e-commerce business will attract and serve customers. Indicate all the channels you plan to leverage to sell physical products in an online space. While it will not be a bricks-and-mortar location, a home office, fulfillment center or storage lockers, and an upgraded website are necessary. Plans should include employee needs and possible automation, functionality, site designs, inventory, cyber security, storage, finance, sales, and marketing. Consider infrastructure, including all equipment necessary to maintain an efficient and effective internal operation. An e-commerce website is the foundation of your business, and getting it right is crucial.

Key Components of a Business Plan

Market Analysis: This part of your business plan is the one that you are probably dreading the most. It is time-consuming and requires research. You should aim to spend an aggregate number of man-hours equivalent to at least one month to complete this section. It goes without saying that this time has to be allocated to different people's schedules and strong communication and leadership are vital to ensure the research is correctly directed. Digging deep into this research will uncover areas that will be essential for your online store to prosper.

Business Description: This is your chance to be proud and explain your online store. You'll also want to paint a clear picture of your store. It can be beneficial to think about what type of industry you're in - are there specific challenges in retail and online retail that are unique to your market?

Executive Summary: Think of an executive summary as a concise version of your business plan. It's essentially the business equivalent of a movie trailer. The purpose of this part of your business plan is to grab the reader's attention and show them exactly what they can expect by reading the rest of your plan.

The next stage of your start-up journey requires you to map out the finer details of your online store. The most important thing to write (before any code) is a full description of your intended business. Although there is no one-size-fits-all answer to what should be in your business plan, the following are the key components that you'll want to include.

CHAPTER 4

Choosing the Right E-Commerce Platform

However, WooCommerce's weaknesses are equally visible. First and foremost, the performance is poor. It scores poorly on the three main e-commerce performance indexes: First Byte, Start Render, and Page Load. This is primarily due to WordPress' poor ability at dividing and coordinating resources, like sending 50 SQL queries for four product pictures on separate pages. There are also more than 4,000 plugins designed for WooCommerce, of which some are poorly programmed and conflicting with each other easily. It is often the case that after a site is built and starts to grow, it takes about $40 per month for a WooCommerce online store to use the plugins it really needs. Lastly, WooCommerce has strict theme requirements. Many premium themes are built to sell regardless of their usability.

So why would anyone still choose WordPress? The biggest reason is certainly that a WooCommerce setup is easy. In fact, the setup page allows the inexperienced to launch their first online store without a hitch. There are also a great number of themes available, of which some stand out because of their beautiful design. Furthermore, ever since WooCommerce turned three, it has become a mature product with an increasingly strong support plan.

One of the most popular platforms in the world for small and medium-sized websites is WordPress, which still has strong e-commerce capabilities through plugins, especially the world-famous WooCommerce. While it is relatively inexpensive to build an online store through WordPress, other platforms not only provide a more comprehensive range of plugins and themes, support more products, allow for customization, and are less buggy, but also make it convenient for non-techies to manage.

A caption to build an online store is what a foundation is to a house. To ensure the success of your e-commerce website, choose the right platform to house your online store. While you may choose to engage a website design company to help you build your website, choosing the right e-commerce platform can make or break your entire business.

Comparison of Popular E-Commerce Platforms

The factors you should consider are your budget, the level of technical knowledge you have about the subject, the degree of customization you would like to conduct on your online store itself, and the payment methods you will be offering. All e-commerce platforms operate on a monthly licensing fee. The only non-monthly licensing fee involved solution is using a shopping cart software, where you will have to pay for it once and do the installation and configuration by yourself. Some of the more user-friendly e-commerce platforms are: Shopify, Bigcommerce, and Volusion. If you are looking for more customization and offers payment methods like Paypal, Amazon or 2CheckOut, you should try using Magento.

You are ready to decide which e-commerce platform you will be using to power your own online store. Deciding on the best e-commerce platform is the most crucial step in starting your online store. If you select the right one, you will be able to build your online store quickly and efficiently. If you select the wrong software, you will not only waste time but you will also have to pay licensing fees for another software if you decide to change.

CHAPTER 5

Setting Up Your Online Store

Clearly, one advantage is that you can reach anyone in the world. But there are others. In the first chapter, we talked about definitions, advantages, the history, and the future of the ecommerce market. The second chapter was about business models. The third chapter was about the different players in the ecommerce market. In this chapter, we are going to talk about what you need to do so you can start your own ecommerce. We are going to explain the steps you need to take so you can set up your own online store. This part is about how you can use the knowledge you got from the previous chapters so you can plan and execute your ecommerce.

Even if you have a regular physical or "brick-and-mortar" store, you need to have your online store. Studies have shown that consumers use the internet to get information about products before purchasing. By having both a store, you cater to all sorts of people: those who want to check the merchandise in person, and those who want to shop from the comfort of their home. But that is only one reason why you should have an online store. There are others just as compelling.

Domain Name Registration and Hosting

As mentioned in the previous chapter, if you are willing to spend a small amount of money on building your online store, and expect to get professional results, it is better to register your own domain name. Having a unique, easily searchable and memorable domain name that reflects what you are selling will always lend a more professional appearance to your online store. These are web addresses that look like "www.mycompany.com," where "mycompany" is the unique part of the address, and ".com" is just one of the possible suffixes or top-level domains (TLDs). Other common suffixes are ".net", ".org", and ".edu" and some TLDs are country specific like ".uk" (United Kingdom), ".de" (Germany), and ".ca" (Canada). Marketing research has shown that most people usually have a hard time recognizing a domain that isn't a .com domain and if they know the site name but don't quite remember it, they usually try to add ".com" to the name, thus giving the .com domain name owner an edge.

Once you have decided what your online store will look like and which software you would like to use for your store, the next step is to identify what you will need in terms of hosting and support, and choose a domain name. These sections will help you understand what these concepts are, and help you identify what is best for your online store.

Designing Your Storefront

Then, finally, you're ready to take the stage and style the rest of your elements. Remember: a great store isn't built in a day and all successful businesses have a custom storefront.

Second, almost every single site component can and should be customized with your color palette and logo - from buttons to line styles to drop downs to backgrounds to zoom lightboxes to social icons and basically anything you can zoom in on using my zooming superpower. Make your site yours and give it a good and original look.

Before you get started on making your store look as beautiful as you envision, there are some visual aspects to consider. First, you need to think about the overall look and feel of your site. Ask yourself, what adjectives do you want people to use when describing it? Bold? Minimalist? Traditional? Trendy? Fun? Determining this early in the shopping process will keep your site consistent. The last thing you want is to have confusing messaging around what your site or your products are about.

CHAPTER 6

Product Sourcing and Inventory Management

Finding the right supplier is a challenge for companies with inventory, as the challenge is striking a balance between the cost of goods and the ability to meet the needs of the customer at the right time. In this chapter, we will discuss how to manage inventory with the different problems, costs, and characteristics that are present, and some techniques to maintain optimal inventory levels. In reference to the other components of product sourcing, there are factors also present when dealing with the points of location, quality, and price – including how to determine the right product, calculating how much you should pay, and ensuring that you meet legal requirements.

Mismanagement of inventory consistently represents 35-45% of losses associated with retail businesses failing within a five-year time period. Not carrying enough inventory for high demand can lose customers to competitors and result in a loss of profit. Holding onto excess inventory can also be costly, as it marks a loss over time. Time is also another dimension of managing inventory because an article of inventory can only be in one place at a time. An article in storage cannot be sold; in the same way, an article not in storage but in the shop display cannot be delivered to a buyer. Time is important because opportunity costs play a role in shopping, business, and handling inventory.

Dropshipping vs. Holding Inventory

The traditional model involves purchasing the products at wholesale prices in advance and holding the inventory in anticipation of receiving an order. When a customer places an order on your website, you ship the merchandise to your customer. The advantages of holding inventory include higher profit margins, more control over the fulfillment process, and the ability to inspect the merchandise before it's shipped. The disadvantages include having to tie up your credit card line and warehouse space. With the traditional model, you need to purchase inventory and/or invest time in creating inventory (in the case of digital products). Then store the items and take care of shipping when an order comes in.

Dropshipping involves an agreement to carry and ship inventory on behalf of the merchant. When a dropshipper customer places an order on your website, you place the same order with the supplier and the supplier ships the merchandise to your customer. The advantages of dropshipping include not having to carry inventory and ship it yourself, not having to tie up your credit with inventory, less risk, and fewer capital requirements. The disadvantages include lower profit margins and a lack of control over the fulfillment process, which can sometimes result in poor service to your customers.

CHAPTER 7

Payment Gateways and Security

For those of you using a Third-Party Store: The gateway comes included in the shopping cart. If a service wants to charge you extra to process your credit card orders, walk away. There are a few factors to take into consideration when choosing a credit card gateway. First, you will likely have the option between using a service that won't store your credit card data or one that will. If you use a service that doesn't store your customer's credit card data, fewer laws apply, and you save yourself the potential problems of a big-time hack. If the service does store the customer information, when the company is hacked, as some companies inevitably are, you are going to feel the pain of government investigations, and you will get to deal with this squad. Your business will go through a lot of headache that it may not survive. When Target was hacked during Christmas of 2013, one-fourth of their revenue vanished, and they were left swimming in bad press, lawsuits, and insurmountable headaches. This is what can happen to your company, even if you use a reputable third party. It happened to the hotel I used to work for when our Merchant was hacked. Not only do you not want this to happen, you don't want to have to deal with the potential legal fees that come with the fiascos that third parties are likely to have. With the hacks on Target, Sony, and other big companies over the past few years, the government is going to have to do something about the theft, especially since the Target hack compromised 110 million people's information. To mitigate the loss in the case of a hack that affects you, I would also suggest Merchant Coverage. If the bank makes this an optional fee or uses a third party to provide this service, GO WITH THE THIRD PARTY. I've always heard ClassicMerchant is good at this. As suggested, to make sure that third parties are keeping their promise, double-check any ratings and reviews that you come across. The best option is to use a third-party credit card processor and Gateway combined, such as PayPal, Visa, MasterCard in a Box, or QuickBooks. With the third-party credit card processor and Gateway, security is generally very strong, and identity theft becomes a large distance less likely to happen. When selecting a third-party credit card processor, take time to learn about each one's security features and the resources they have available to members if the worst-case scenario happens to you.

 This is the most important aspect of creating and maintaining your store. After all, you're in business to make money, and if you make it difficult for your customers to pay, they won't. A payment gateway is something that most people don't ever consider, even when they have seen a demonstration of what it is. I suppose that it's so seemingly intuitive that it's thought to be a no-brainer. It's simply "The Shopping Cart." However, a custom shopping cart that fits seamlessly inside your site isn't as easy to come by as you may think. There are plenty of third-party shopping carts available, but they don't necessarily mesh with the 'look' of your site. There are a couple of sites that will charge you money to link their shopping carts to your site. These are quite frequently cost-prohibitive and are meant for heavier traffic than you are likely to receive in your first years of operation.

Choosing a Payment Gateway

There are three main categories of instruments used in payment processing: everyone's familiar with credit and debit cards, as well as a more traditional method of selling products – checks. Today, checks are usually processed electronically and converted into a digital format for transmission over the network. In the background, this all involves transactions between banks, the most important partners in this type of payment instrument. And the preferred method is electronic payment (e-payment) which many users find convenient and fast. In addition, e-payments are safer than traditional postal mail or carrier modes; usually, e-payments require some type of security sign-in to prove the payer's identity.

One of the most important aspects of your online store's setup is choosing the right payment processor to handle customer transactions. Numerous different payment processors exist, with the major share of the market divided among a handful of companies. Payment processors will take a small fee from every transaction they process for you. Yet when choosing a payment processor, you shouldn't merely focus on their fees. Payment processors have different product offerings and vary in terms of pricing and features. Depending on which payment processor you choose, you may have access to services like fraud and chargeback protection, in-store point of sale support, or instant transfers to your bank account.

Implementing Secure Payment Systems

This type of automatic approval is crucial for the type of store where people shop when stores are closed - online stores.

When you go to a store and pay for your purchases by credit card, the merchant uses this terminal to verify the credit card.

The account is credited by the credit card company, the merchant is informed that the account has been credited, and a receipt is printed. All of the details of the transaction are forwarded to the merchant's acquiring bank, which passes the details on to the credit card company. Banks keep track of which merchants have access to this technology, and they adjust the credit limit for the merchant on a daily basis if needed.

We were a bit skeptical when we first heard about selling easy payments processing to online merchants. The state-of-the-art for such services today is that merchants can sign up from a website and be accepting credit card payments, complete with automatic transaction processing, merchant tracking of all transactions, detailed monthly statements, etc. within 48 hours. The infrastructure that allows us to do this is mainly the ubiquitous credit card point of sale terminals in use worldwide.

CHAPTER 8

Marketing and Customer Acquisition

This is also the most nebulous and complex of the obstacles to building a new business. While the internet can have you in touch with potential customers in minutes, that doesn't mean that you will have their attention for more than seconds. Thus, your marketing efforts aren't just a simple "Send" key away, but rather a huge bucket of activities that you have to start throwing one at a time. Only after having so many of them in motion that you're in a whirlwind of advertising and PR promotions will you have a steady stream of sales, and only when you have woven the majority of them together into your day-to-day work will you have a runaway success.

When you launch your store to the world, the biggest challenge you'll face is making people aware that you exist. Even with the best product at the best price, no one will shop at your store if they don't know it's there. This is marketing, and it is the most important part of your business next to having high-quality merchandise at a competitive price. A store with poor merchandise and good marketing can do alright. A store with no marketing will fail.

Search Engine Optimization (SEO)

The traditional channel of interpersonal relationships, supported by the outer world, affects the growth of new customers, old buyers, and loyalty. The presence of a well-created company account is also important. Make a good overview, product description, contacts, photos, terms of payment, description, and playlist. The company is its top management, activity, environment, and target audience in social networks. Reliability, accuracy, responsibility - these are the qualities that you as a company want to see on the part of other market participants. Establish relationships with service users, solve problems, answer questions, and collect testimonials. With the audience, relationship management can also be marketing research, promotional activities, and business announcements.

You need accessibility and an easy way to buy your selected product or service. "How do I make a purchase?" This is a difficult and urgent question for online shoppers. Keeping a purchase is tough, so do everything you can to make it easier for customers to buy. To do this, you need an easy-to-understand sales funnel, a clear hierarchical structure, a clear basket, and an application form. Prices, discounts, and delivery, fast loading, good descriptions. Create a unique and user-friendly website in style and quick loading.

Writing on a blog is the most profitable content method. There are many reasons for this, but the main ones are loyalty to visitors and their conversion into buyers. Articles on the site do not directly sell, but they create the necessary reputation, inform, and entertain visitors. Collaboration with companies, niche bloggers, PR production, texts about the company. The strategy with blogs consists of attracting the blogger's audience to the business.

Search engine optimization is a gradual process. First of all, you need to decide on the semantic core. The semantic core is a full list of keywords that characterize your online store. These are words, phrases, sentences that people type in search engines to find products that you have.

Optimizing your online store to get free traffic from search engines is incredibly powerful. First of all, you have to understand that 70-80% of Google buyers look for products through the top three links. Only 20-30% get to the fourth link and below. Also, the conversion rate for search engine traffic is much higher than for other marketing channels. Imagine, the search engine visitor knows what he needs, looks for it, finds it, and buys it. Therefore, the basic rule is to enter the top three, that's where the big money is.

Social Media Marketing Strategies

Ask promotional accounts to feature your products Reach out to different niche-related influencers and ask them to feature your products. Some will do it for free; others will ask for money, especially if they have a big, active, and engaged audience. Find the ones that have a good fit with your niche and collaborate with them to promote your products effectively.

Use relevant, high-traffic hashtags Instagram allows up to 30 hashtags in the caption and comments. Spend some time doing hashtag research and testing to see which ones are the most effective in your niche. Use high-traffic hashtags, but make sure not to overuse them, as Instagram might penalize you or even block your account.

Check out and comment on the major brands and influencers in your niche. Post comments under their images. Don't forget to include a link to your profile so that people can see your store and start following you if they like your comment. Be an active member in the chosen community in order to market your products effectively.

CHAPTER 9

Customer Service and Retention

- Clearly Designate an About Us Section: It's sometimes hard to find the contact information from an online store, so you must make your about us section easily accessible from your site. People want to do business with people they can trust, so explaining who and what you are in a couple of sentences shows the customer your trustworthiness as well as a small piece of your personality. - Responsive E-Mail: Make sure that when your customers e-mail you, you respond as quickly as possible. Nothing irks me more than writing someone an endlessly descriptive e-mail and then waiting weeks for a response. - Easy Contact Information: Make sure for all inquiries, the customer knows exactly where to reach you, whether there are questions about a certain product or a refund request. A "contact us" page is the perfect tool to have for sending e-mails or a client service phone number. - Quick Replies: Whenever you receive an inquiry, you should send a quick, helpful reply. Do not let them wait around – people do not want to have to drag information out of you. If they do, they will most likely give their business to someone else. - Clear Communications: Also, your customers do not want to feel like they are being misled, so have clear policies. You should be upfront about your shipping, supplier partnerships, and refund policies. It's also important to include any warranties, product care instructions, and delivery dates. Always be grateful: Since the customer doesn't have to purchase from you, give them reasons to want to. A customer appreciation day that offers them a 20% discount as a thanks for their purchase would earn you points with your customers. - Honor Each Customer Services Agreement: You must have great follow-through. Make sure to follow up and go the extra mile if needed. Customers who feel like they have an easy time when it comes to transactions and information will come back again and again.

In an online store, customer service is incredibly important. This is because the customer can easily drop in and out of your site with a click of a button. That's how easy it is for your customer to change their mind about a purchase. In-person customer service can sometimes make up for it, but when it comes to online stores, service is what makes them come back and purchase more. Here are some tips and ideas for client service:

Effective Communication with Customers

Establish a mechanism, such as a web-based passion forum, through which you can communicate and exchange ideas with your customers, soliciting their input, advising them on products and services, and providing training materials. In order to encourage the effectiveness of the ecommerce initiative, provide a mechanism through which you can establish direct daily interaction and communication with your customers. In your web-based customer service forum, you can provide your customers with rapid responses to queries and product installation or usage questions, as well as suggestions for enhancing your products and services. Provide valuable content, such as interactive training materials, products or services, in order to forge a closer relationship with your customers. There are three features that will help your ecommerce initiative stand out: interactive training materials, forums, and online seminars.

In today's digital economy, success depends on effective electronic communication. In order to develop a positive relationship with your customers, investors, and partners and keep them informed and happy, you must develop and maintain an online presence. You must keep your customers informed of their existing and new needs and periodically solicit their input by allowing your readership to provide feedback.

It is important to establish an open channel of communication with your customers and to maintain it at all times. In order to put your investors at ease and to keep your customers informed, it may be necessary to explain Soundview's challenges online where they can participate.

CHAPTER 10

Analyzing and Optimizing Your Store

Marketing campaigns provide great opportunities to analyze the flow around a website as a visitor journeys from searching for your product or service to leaving the site, order completed or not. Of course, it would be helpful to look at traffic sources and see if anything unusual is happening. If there is more traffic in aggregate, then the ratios you calculate aren't really the "normal" metric you are used to, yet, nobody, except you, really ever calculates that ratio so nothing is lost.

Next, over time there should be a steady pop and level day pattern in these TC metrics. Okay, sometimes promotions influence the shape of the curve and other times promotions don't. That's why you really want to see the normal shape of the curve before promotion and then during the big event to isolate this effect. If there's no discernible pattern, you have bigger problems with your site and the focus should be figuring out what's up.

The second step is to aggregate by the dimension you are thinking of analyzing. Because the page view and visit related metrics are in terms of visitors, you have to sum up the transactions for the same time period by the same dimension to get meaningful results. It would also be helpful to look for other factors potentially influencing your results.

Just to repeat, the first thing is to metric tone what you spent all that time creating. When you get your weekly report, of course you look at revenue and think about your performance against some weekly objective. What are the 3-5 other KPIs you track on your dashboard week to week? If you don't have an answer, stop now, and find out or decide.

Now that you have pages of analytics, it's time to make some decisions about what to do. You have so many more things you could also do, but we will stick to the highest impact activities. Here are the steps to get started.

Key Metrics to Track

Customers do not typically arrive at an online store with the product page bookmarked and ready to go. Most want to browse a little before making a decision. According to sales data from Internet Retailer's 2011 Top 500 Guide, search users typify the most valuable digital shopper. Monetate's E-commerce Quarterly states that search accounts for a 2.49 percent average conversion rate, compared to 1.55 percent for non-searching users. The referred link (search engines and ads) conversion rate from VWO Insights Blog sets search traffic up as a standard-bearer in revenue. Have you known 30 percent of users start searches with search engines, and the other 70 percent browse your store then try to buy products? This gives you a suggestion of what VWO should develop further to fulfill the Search function mission.

You can track Sponsored Products-equipped campaigns through Ad Campaign reports. You can add ref_column1 to the reports and check if there is page information or not. If no page is added, in other words, most people exit immediately, your advertisement has only a disadvantageous effect.

Pull-Out Rate = Total Number of Users Who Click on Ads But Exit the Store Immediately / Total Number of Unique Visitors

Pull-Out Rate is the number of visitors who come to an online store via an advertisement but immediately leave the site. The formula for calculating the pull-out rate is given below.

Conversion Rate Optimization

Key Metrics to Watch Before you start making changes to your site or testing variables to increase your desired outcomes, make sure you have a good handle on various key metrics. Not every e-commerce store has the same goals, so your key metrics might be different than these: What are the conversion rates? This is just the number of actions you want divided by the total number of visits. It gives you a basic sense of who's in control: you or your customers. Also, pay attention to the funnel conversion rate. The funnel conversion rate is how often someone moves through key steps of your site. In most cases, this means going from a visitor to a cart adder to payment information entry to paying. However, funnels can be much more complicated when you have other desired outcomes you're looking to optimize for. The average time on site tells you how long people end up sticking around before they take the desired action. The other thing to pay close attention to is the average order value. This is just the total revenue divided by the number of sales.

After people find your site, visit, and browse around, ideally, they should buy something. And if you've managed to get your products in front of your ideal customers, chances are good they will. However, it's not always that easy to get people to buy something or turn into leads. And that's where conversion rate optimization (CRO) comes in. Your store's conversion rate is the rate at which visitors end up buying something or becoming a lead. CRO involves making changes to your site to increase the rate of people who take the desired action. This can include making changes to your site to ensure your audience doesn't leave before adding items to the cart, enters their payment information, or clicks on an offer. Over time, this can dramatically improve the number of visits you need to get in order to generate a sale.

CHAPTER 11

Scaling Your E-Commerce Business

Start by making the numbers work. When some brand-new e-commerce store owners imagine starting a business, they often look at the nearest success stories and mimic them. What's often not factored into this is that those businesses that are already ultra-successful have gone through a lot to become a huge success. In other words, your current point of view is likely not what you should be basing your goals on. In order to properly scale a business, you have to think big but start small by trying to decrease cost and increase profit at every opportunity. You may have already done this to a certain extent, so keep going down the list with ideas like discounted shipping options, material costs and more. Always be sure to be highlighting and marketing your added value to your customers often and as creatively as you can.

At this point, you've got a pretty healthy e-commerce store built and in operation. What's the next step, other than finding a bigger and better venue to hold your victory party at? That's right, it's time to scale your business. After all, the next obvious step is to get as many eyes on these amazing products or services you've created, so that means it's time to scale. In many cases, in order to hit that next level of success, business owners often have to take that next step in hiring contractors, employees, or even a team to help manage the load. With the right approach, and a solid e-commerce platform to back it up like WooCommerce, you should be set for rapidly accelerated growth. In a way, getting to the point of scaling an e-commerce business is like climbing a rather tall mountain. You need to be a bit strategic about the way you approach things, again relying on a solid team of experts who can truly help you along the way.

Expanding Product Lines

One great thing about an online store is the ease of adding new products. However, this apparent advantage of being able to add new products quickly needs to be viewed in light of the limited attention span of an average customer. There is nothing worse than a huge list of products that nobody can browse through. Be mercenary. Is the cost of showing those products consistent with their expected income? There are costs associated with every product you offer: screen space, mailing list sign-ups, transactions. None of these is very high, but they add up. Remember, when mod_perl or mod_php takes an extra millisecond delivering that huge list of products, it doesn't sound like much, but when you add up ten thousand requests a day over the course of six months, it really does sound substantial, doesn't it?

International Expansion Strategies

In sum, while it can be difficult, implementing successful international growth strategies becomes much easier than ever before via the internet, and doing so can be a cost-effective strategy given the high potential for growth in online international retailing.

As e-commerce continues to thrive in the US market, retailers need to focus on their international sales. International expansion can be a cost-effective strategy to grow your revenue stream. Major questions that online retailers need to consider are: Will consumers from different countries crave my products? Which customer services are critical to the consumers of various countries? Should I use in-country currency for transactional processes?

CHAPTER 12

Legal and Compliance Considerations

If you have an existing business, selling goods, for example, in a bricks and mortar store, you should ensure that the establishment of an online store is not in breach of any lease. If you have signed a lease, you need to ensure that the lease refers to sales from any online store and/or you obtain consent from the landlord (if necessary) to sell goods from an online store.

In your online store, you should have a delivery policy, setting out how long it will take for goods to be delivered and whether you charge customers for delivery. The time period set out in any policy should be reasonable and a violation of your delivery timeframe may offend consumer laws as to misleading and deceptive conduct.

You should do your best to ensure that the personal data of your customers, which they provide to you when purchasing goods from your online store, is kept private. You should review our Privacy Policy to ensure that it complies with the Privacy Act 1988 (Cth).

You may decide to accept returns in relation to the goods you sell in your online store. You may also be required to provide a refund if the goods are not of merchantable quality or are not fit for their intended purpose. The sale of goods may also be covered by warranties required to be given by law. You should ensure that if you decide to accept returns, you have a returns policy and also a policy relating to any refunds that may be due under law, for example, if the goods are faulty.

Privacy Policies and Terms of Service

Another good thing to have on your website is a terms of service. This is not required like a privacy policy, but it can be used to clarify and limit your legal liability. It can also be used to set ground rules for users to abide by on the site. Online store hosts, like our company, offer options for having either of these but do not tailor them specifically to your online store, so you should consider consulting with a legal professional for the most accurate and legitimate content.

When creating an online store or website, it is necessary, sometimes required by law, to have a privacy policy. The privacy policy is a description of what data you store and what you use it for on your site. For example, if you keep people's email and use it to send them emails about limited time sales or new products, you should have a privacy policy that users can read to know that their email is being used for marketing purposes. Having this policy is also the law in some countries. There are a variety of resources online with examples of templates and guides to creating such a policy. With our ecommerce hosting sites, we also offer an option for a CSV of all of the user data you have stored on your website. Just let us know that you need this file and we can send it to you!

CHAPTER 13

Conclusion and Next Steps

Find the right products for your store and start reaching out to suppliers where necessary to source those products. If you start prepping your store early, you'll find many of the suppliers will be happy to also push the store to their customers, as any extra business is good business for them. Get in touch with the community for moral support and early business. If you're worried about telling people that you're working on your store, direct friends and family to the 'holding page' which can be set up in minutes, and ask for email signups from anyone that visits. Start using Google to research who your ideal audience is and what they find memorable. Any questions, support and supplementary reading? Please get in touch as always.

In conclusion, this guide should give you everything you need to launch your fantasy store. Any upcoming chapters you believe would further help do this, please let me know and I can add them in. Next steps are below. Good luck and I hope I've helped.

Final Tips for Success

Many aspects are important for an online shop to survive in the market. In today's competitive world, marketing strategies play a particular role in online store functionality. The daily mandate is to anticipate, learn, develop novel strategic changes, and therefore increase the advancements in the marketplace. In this way, the growing competition in the market can be met, and the potential buyer can stick to a given brand or product. It is a constant challenge but a big part of organizational development.

Enhance the credibility of your company by providing a high-quality and secure product. Highlight the links to your policies, terms, and conditions on each product page so that customers find them easily and quickly. Offer a post-sale satisfaction guarantee. Trust in the quality of your products and give your customers time to receive, use, and appreciate them. Offer a toll-free return policy to help customers feel safe when shopping. Finally, always upgrade your sales, control maintenance, advertise your online store, and insert links to your site on external websites. As the site grows, online marketing techniques, such as organic search traffic, will become increasingly important.

To ensure the success of your business, we have developed some final tips for you to consider. First, make sure that your website has easy navigation and a great search. Additionally, your website should be visually appealing, so be sure to gather a variety of pictures of your products to direct the attention of consumers. Brand quality has become a priority in today's online store. Offer superior customer service, including different types of customer service (e-mail, phone, chat, Facebook, and Twitter). Use creative marketing to differentiate your online store from other companies. Your company must create a brand capable of attracting your customer.

Milton Keynes UK
Ingram Content Group UK Ltd.
UKHW040808160724
445389UK00004B/239